World of Dragons
and Other Timely Frustrations:

A Collection of (self) Righteous Poetry

Fairchild

Four Doors
Publishing

Copyright © 2025 David Fairchild

ISBN 978-1-960390-10-3

All rights reserved. No part of this publication may be reproduced, stored in a retrieval system, or transmitted in any form or by any means, electronic, mechanical, recording or otherwise, without the prior written permission of the author or artistic contributors.

Cover Art by Isaac Adams

Illustrations by Isaac Adams, Tami Mattinson, Bailey Bird, Chandra Gooding, Matt Trujillo and Stanley Petrovich

Graphic design by Salmon Kristi, Jason Mitchell and David Fairchild

Photography by Trina Tipton and David Fairchild

Glass blowing by Isaiah Hossein

Four Doors Publishing

Spanish Fork, UT 84660

Printed in the United States of America.

Dedication:

This book is dedicated to my friends and students who ran, fled and hid on Sept. 10, 2025. It is dedicated to those who helped me heal and to those who healed alongside me. It is for those who loaned me their strength for the classroom, especially:

Claire, Ava, Anna, Erin, Alyssa, Carson, Shyla, Sean, Josh, Dallan, Tyler, Kayden, Jason, Bridger, Mattthew, Mitt, Kealohi, Elizabeth, Brianne, and Samantha.

Thank you.

Finally, it is dedicated to all of those allies who, alongside me, had to endure the political and disrespectful agenda that followed and spewed forth by people looking to score points and favor rather than practice humanity and compassion.

And for those who are still looking to score those points, I suppose this collection wouldn't exist without you either, but you can go thank yourselves instead. You're pretty good at that. I guess this collection is really for you.

Table of Contents:

Dear Reader 1
Invocation 3
Dear Traditionally Published Author . . . 4
Words. 5
Little Black Marks 6
Sticks 8
Orange 9
Crickets 10
Ten Nommandments 12
Crimson Tide 13
My Playground was Better 14
Curriculum. 15
The Decay. 16
Valedictorian. 18
Flush 20
Empty Rooms 21
World of Dragons 22
A Childrens' Story. 23
For Beatitudes and Spacious Skies . . 31
Wood Coaster Rhythm. 32

Prisoner LCCN 31035230	34
Why the People	36
Nation of Laws	38
Life Logic	40
Sticks and Stones	41
Heroes	42
Influencer	44
Beware, All Ye Who Enter	45
Colors of Hell	46
The Bell	48
Spectacles	50
Human Shield	51
Change in Melody	52
Heavenly Pickets	54
Pop Quiz	56
Light at the End of the Tunnel	57
Try	58
Benediction	60

Dear reader,

    I beg you forgive my ineptitude, for I am no poet.

    If I ever find myself burning in hell, it will most likely be with me sitting behind a cold, steel desk having to write poetry with a fountain pen that spits my ink everywhere and has to be refilled after every stroke. I have words elsewhere, in strength and publication, where I have more power in creating imagery as only words can. But this is not one of those places. This is more like a path in purgatory for me.

    In fact, I have long sworn that, if there is a piece of writing that I would never publish, it would be a body of poetry. For that requires a skill, of which I have none, and demands a tongue and vocabulary that I lack. Like a broken bottle of molasses that dries in the kitchen cabinet, I am too profane and vulgar to keep this craft beautiful and holy.

    Some may ask, why write it then? All I can say is that on Sept. 10 of 2025, an assassin invaded my home at Utah Valley University and shot and killed Charlie Kirk in front of the students whom I encouraged to go and attend his event. One shot rang out, but the screams and the footsteps that filled the campus will forever scar the halls that have long been my sanctuary.

    Yet, it is what came after that truly mocked our community, as people who had never set foot on our campus began to turn our tragedy into their political megaphone. While we, who were there, struggled to heal, political buffoonery rubbed salt in our wounds.

It was compounded by the shouting of people who claimed to be religious and Christian while behaving in unchristian-like manner, stirring hate and contention and pretending it was good—even giving my own faith a bad name. As a lifelong Christian, I have found it to be a source of embarrassment.

As I endured hearing the ramblings of insensitive people, I realized even poetically-inept tongues could be loosened. Whether one should call what flows from mine as poetry, I dare not say. For what do I know about poetry?

And so, I ask your indulgence as you must endure my unintelligent ramblings and the screams of my soul, as it shakes in pain at logic and people and crosses and more that could use a good slap sometimes. I don't mean any slap. I mean the kind mothers used to employ to ward off buffoonery. I think perhaps this collection of frustrations is paltry effort on my part to work through my list grievances, guilt and small discovery of joy. Strange for you, but I think less so for me. After all, I'm not the one who has to read it.

Again, my apologies. Enjoy.

Invocation:

Stand or You Will be Removed

Our Father which art in heaven,
Hallowed be thy name.
Thy Kingdom come and will be done,
but it better be our way!
Forgive us all our dues,
and give us our daily bread
by making people feed us,
while we enforce new debts.
Lead us not into temptation,
but deliver us from evil.
For thine is the kingdom, power, and glory.
And we feast on it like weevils.

Ame….
You know what.
Just hurry up.
We've been righteous long enough.

Dear traditionally published author:
(an Americanized haiku)

If I have to read
another craptastic hit,
I'm gonna punch you!

Signed,

An independent author.

Words

Words.　　　　Words.
Your words.　　My words.
Two halves joined in our words,
　beating strength among us.
　　Syllabic in pum-PuMP!
　　　Our language
　　　　and veins
　　　　　pulse.
　　　　　You.　　　　　　Me.
　　　　　　　　　　　　Shame!
　　　　　　　　　　On my words!
　　　　　　　　　Nicked your veins.
　　　　　　　Your veins in my heart,
　　　　　grown in to refresh my soul.
　　　　Ingrained, invested, circulatory.
　　　　Sliced with　　　a scalpel:
　　　　　Words.　　　　Now
　　　　　　　　　　　　　b
　　　　　　　　　　　　　l
　　　　　　　　　　　　　e
　　　　　　　　　　　　　e
　　　　　　　　　　　　　d
　　　　　　　　　　　　　i
　　　　　　　　　　　　　n
　　　　　　　　　　　g out. . . pain:
　　　　broken, hurting. Puddling! Words. Wasteful
　　words. Not yours. Mine. Your veins are we. Beg you,
　　　　　　reseal. Please, forgive me.

Little, Black Marks

When I was little I didn't know words.
I knew black spots, lines and dots and smudges:
splotches.
But splotches, I knew, told a story
of Raggedy Ann and Andy going to the zoo.
Every day the same, going to the zoo.
"Read it again."
"Okay."
"Read it again."
"Again?"
"Read it again."
"Why don't we read something else."
"Read it again."
I looked at the stampings,
marks I didn't know.
Copied each curve, each blot, each slope.
Plagiarized my first story.
"Those are words," she was smart.
She was snotty.
I was older. She could read.

Read to me through her window:
The Gingerbread Man.
"Read it again."
The story was in the black marks.
Told my kindergarten teacher:
"The Gingerbread Man!"
So, she read to us *The Gingerbread Man.*
We got in line, took a journey—
like the gingerbread man—
down the halls,
to the kitchen.
We watched the cook make
a giant gingerbread man.
"Come back in two hours," he said.
"And we'll try to catch him."
But Ray snuck out and caught that gingerbread man.
Ruined the cake. Ruined that book.
The next day he pulled out his tooth
at show-and-tell just to prove that he could.
Bled everywhere!
Wouldn't stop!
I wanted to tell about Raggedy Ann and Andy
at the zoo
and show their black marks.
But Ray's gums gushed all over that hope.
He patted himself on the back and said he did a good job,
believed everyone loved it.
I didn't get to show and tell,
but I learned what an idiot was.
Thought I'd never know an idiot like that again,
who could censor little black marks.

I was wrong.

Sticks

I.

I am a child of God!
And I'm holier than thou
and Thou.

So, I'll use my cross—
which is bigger than yours—
to crack you over the head.
And make you learn
I'm the righteous one
who'll survive great days of dread.

I am a child of God!
And you'd better learn it well,
or I'll beat you down
with my royal crown
and my church that's bigger than hell.

I am a child of God,
and I hold all the clout.
For, remember what the
Good book says:
"It's my way,
or I'll smack you out."

II.

I am a child of God.
And you've read the manual wrong.
The cross is God's firm symbol
of truth, hope, love, and song.
It's a source of inspiration
to lift us all in class.
Which I'm sure you'd get to know,
if you'd pull it from your... mass!

Orange

I used to like orange
before the fake flavor,
all the little pits,
and that permanent, sour pucker on your face.

I used to like orange
when that tarty savor
didn't give me the shits,
and I could throw that bitter peel in its place—

the trash!
With the rest of everything rotten,
decayed and old,
I could drag it to the street for the truck.

Alas!
The garbage man's forgotten.
The pickup is on hold.
So, sadly—with the orange—I am stuck.

Now, black vans fill the streets
while drivers' serenade,
"we love the peel."
And they're too proud to understand that it's bitter.

And they lob out the sweet meat
like tariff war grenades,
'cause they feel
all their neighbors owe them better.

Yet only cause they hear
the orange peel yell—
which sounds like Berkowitz's dog—
and the people at the trough all scream, "hooray!"

And they give no thought to bear
that the orange was made in hell.
And anyone who eats it will get bogged
with a bout of diarrhea that won't end for days and days and days.

Crickets

Too many people say, "I love you."
Seems most don't know what it means.
To some it means, "You complete me;"
to others, "You make me smile;"
to some, "I would die for you;"
while others, "I would live."
"I love you more than life," and
"I need you by my side—
cliché and weak and naïve,
that everyone says when they're greedy.
Some say it without words,
nod of the head while in bed,
a cuddle,
a touch,
a kiss.
And then you roll away.

True, one who loves says it.
But one who loves—
really loves—
knows when not to say it.
Some call it cowardice.

Few call it bravery.
Cowardice screams, "I love you,"
instead of, "Pick me, not him."
That's selfish,
conceited,
a hail Mary, full of grace.
Bravery holds "I love you" back
for when she finds another,
and you know she deserves joy.
And, yet, you're still alone.
True love is when you can sustain
that she's not yours,
and hide that it kills you
so you don't frighten her away,
and lose her all together.
Love isn't stalking.
it's staying away.
Love isn't giving in,
it's refraining.
Love isn't, "I love you."
it's, "I'm glad you're happy."
And you mean it.
Love is being able to say it,
and know it's unfair to hear it back.
Hearts in love beat
and through forces unseen,
maybe quantum,
maybe God,
the hearts feel the other's pulse.

And when that rhythm becomes quiet,
it knows one is happy,
or dying.

"I love you," is not words.
It's life. It's blood.
It fills your veins,
never leaves.
It's in your thoughts all day;
makes your nightly wishes and prayers;
fills your dreams;
saddens your mornings.
Long drives, remind you.
Music makes you cry,
especially when someone else
is playing that one song.
Skies scream crayon blue into your brain,
nights remind you, everything is black.
And crickets laugh at your misery.

Time doesn't heal it.
Only presence does,
worse than drugs.
Love is dwindling of hope
when she's gone,
and worse the longer she's gone.

Time doesn't heal it.
Only presence does,
worse than drugs.
Love is dwindling of hope
when she's gone,
and worse the longer she's gone.

And whn you find the one
that can make you forget
this is love too
and she picks you,
that's an even better song.

Love doesn't need to say what it is.
Perhaps one could say it's survival.
Perhaps one might say that it's love.
Too many people are saying it though,
And too many don't really know.

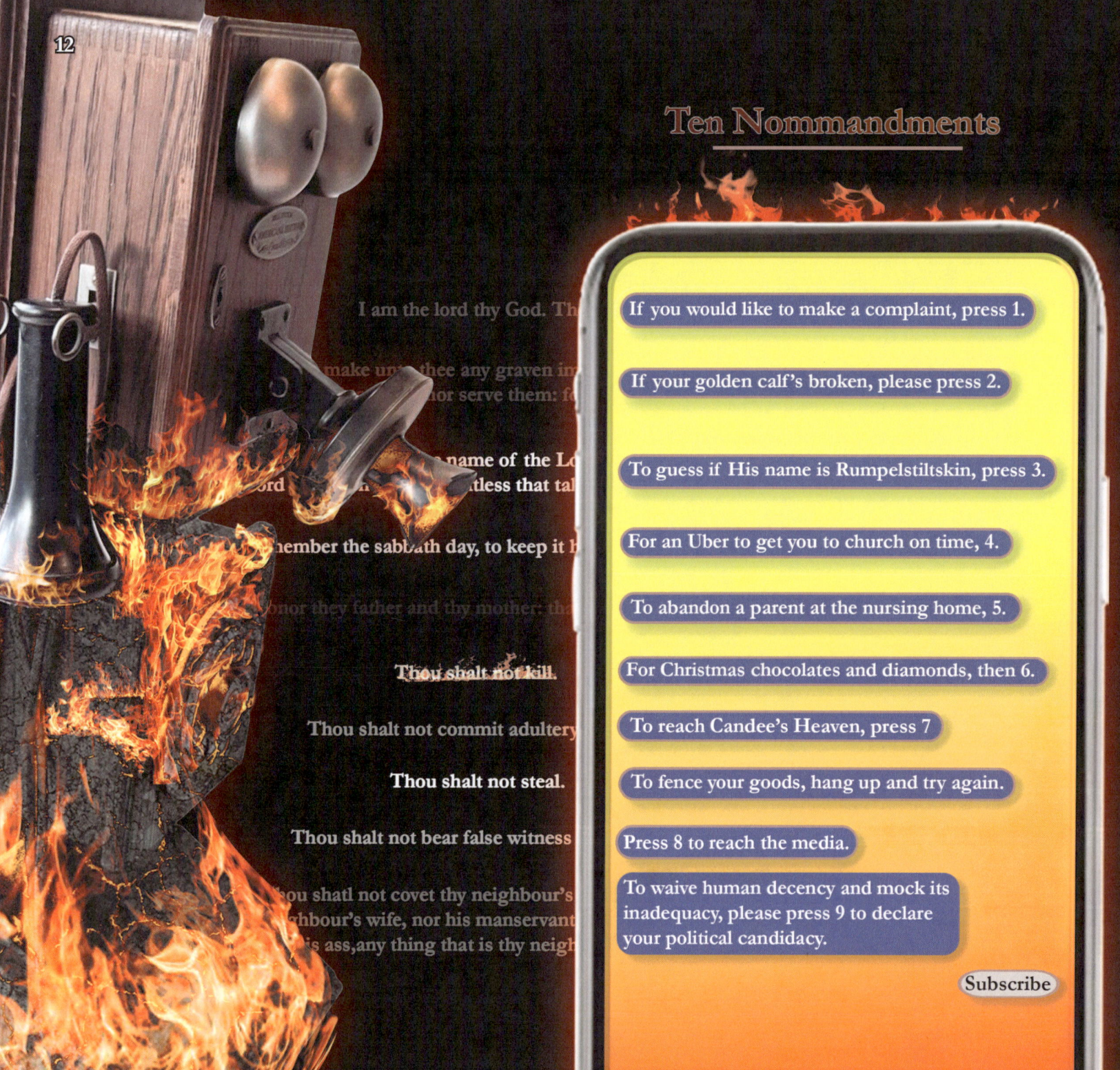

Crimson Tide

A woman stood on the beach, as the masks rolled in.
As the masks rolled in, they drowned her flame.
They drowned her flame, and she called them fools.
And she called them fools: "don't you ride those waves!"
"Don't you ride those waves," she shouted and screamed.
She shouted and screamed at the faceless waves—
at the faceless waves. They wore cowards' masks!
They wore cowards' masks as they rolled back in.
As they rolled back in, the woman cried.
The woman cried, "that's not fair!"
That's not fair," the woman complained.
The woman compained. The waves were there.
The waves were there; the masks didn't care.
The masks didn't care a woman stood on the beach.

My Playground was Better Than Yours

My playground was better than yours.
And we knew how use it.
We had no upgrades, updates, virus protection—

We had swings. We had rockets.
We had tires for spelunking.
We had grass. We had pavement.
We had metal spiderwebs.
We had Red Rover

And sometimes, grown-ups carried whistles.

We rode on creatures that bounced on springs.
We spun carousels that threw us off.
Awesome! Because girls talked to us
when they signed our casts.

We mashed fields filled with giant teams.

We fell from see-saws and trees;
played in all sorts of paint;
balanced on chin-up bars and monkey bars;
and every day had a fight
with jerks who crowded the slides.
Because we all wanted to ride.

We climbed fences you weren't supposed to,
'cuz on the other side
someone would shoot you with rock salt.
That made for a fun game too.

Then one day, whiney parents showed up.

Curriculum

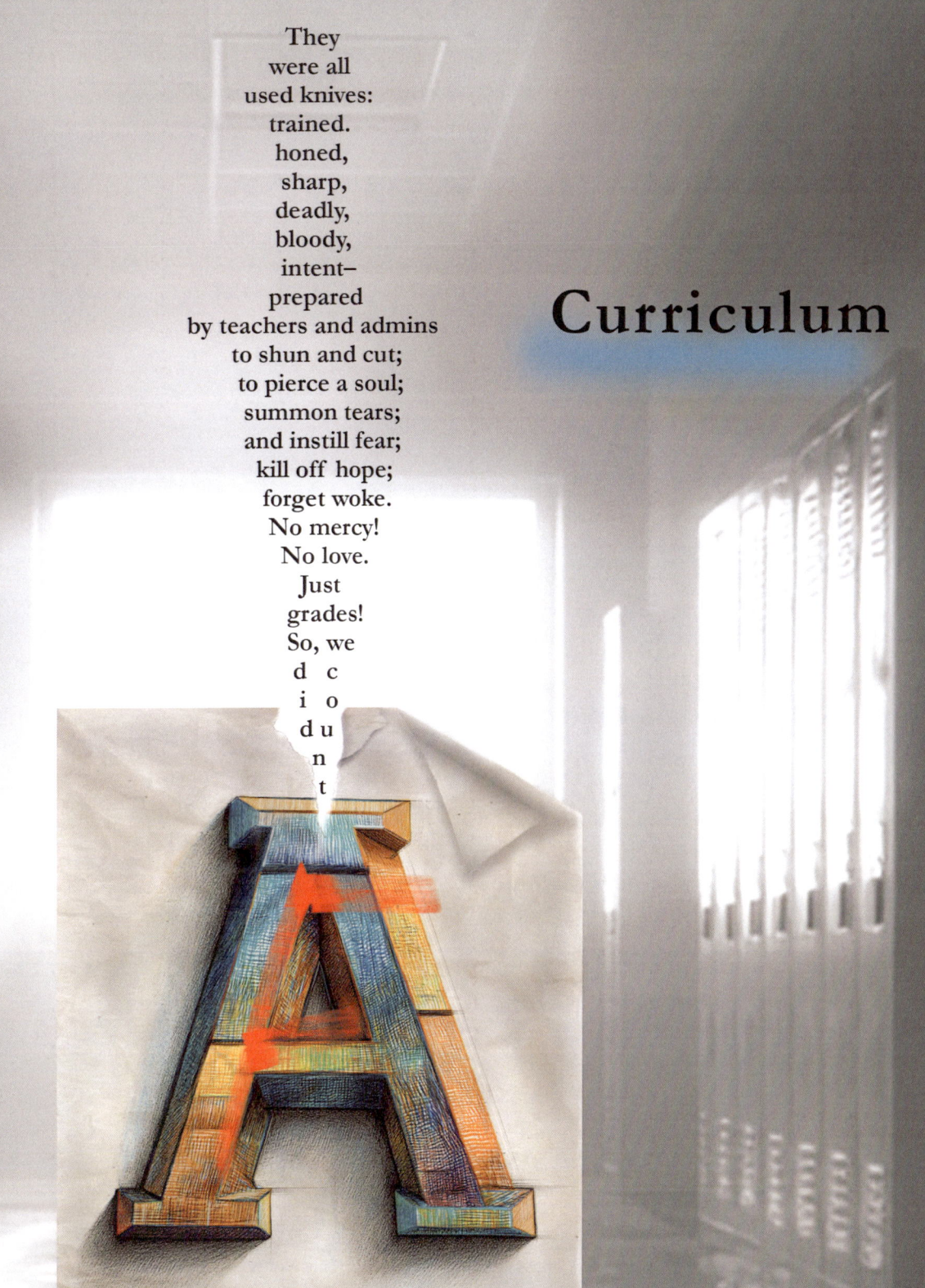

They
were all
used knives:
trained.
honed,
sharp,
deadly,
bloody,
intent—
prepared
by teachers and admins
to shun and cut;
to pierce a soul;
summon tears;
and instill fear;
kill off hope;
forget woke.
No mercy!
No love.
Just
grades!
So, we
did count

Kindergarten:
Learned to write the letters in my name.

First grade:
Read in the highest reading group.
"Can I read this?"
"Sure, honey, read what you want."
        That was my teacher.

Second grade:
Top reading level.
"Can I read this?"
"Whatever. Read what you want."
        Teacher lasted a year.

Third grade:
Top reading level.
"Can I read this?"
"Not until you learn to read with expression."
        I miss her.

Fourth grade:
Top reading level.
"Here's my typewriter. Write me a story."
        That was my teacher.

Fifth grade:
Top reading level.
Teacher thinks something's wrong with me.
"He's depressed."
That was some guy who
Asked me to draw him a picture.
"It's from my How-to-draw book."
Then my teacher.
"Now, test him for slow class."

Special ed teacher told him:
"Stop wasting our time!"
I ask, "can I read this?"
And he says I have to do my dictation.

Sixth grade:
Top reading level,
and teacher cares again.

Seventh grade:
Bored.
Did it all before.
"You'll amount to nothing."
                          That was my teacher.

Eighth grade:
"Can I read this?"
"No, read what's on the list."

Ninth grade:
"Can I read this?"
"No! Read what's on the list!"

Tenth grade:
"Read Shakespeare and love it!"
"Like this?"
"No. You're wrong. You're wrong.
You'll always be wrong!"

God!

Eleventh grade:
          — dropped out.

Valedictorian

Austen, Fowles, Harper, Fitch.
T*he Color Purple, Rape Girl, Flowers in the Attic,*
Medievel Literature—
Chaucer!
And all their critical theory.
Creative Writing:
Theresa's detailed short story of losing her virginity,
whether I wanted to know it or not.
Biography Writing 3050:
Angelou's Caged Bird, Sebold's *Lucky*.
"Can I please read something else?"
"Why?"
"I'm sick of reading about rape and incest."
"Well that's literature."
"No, that's SOME literature."
"You read it! You read it and you like it! Or no A!"
"You take it and you read it, or no A!"
Even in creative writing,
when the personal biographies of other students came!
This classmate raped. That pupil molested.
Every woman in class molested or raped!
Some of their babies molested or raped.
All of them, except one.
She enjoys graphic sex on the stairs and thinks
I care about his tongue and her lips—
not those ones. Then plot twist! It was rape.
My biography piece was about overcoming stage fright
After being sabotaged in a show.
I got an F. Why? Ask Maya.
Next assignment, please!
Now, every woman wrote about being a rape victim.
I wrote about a college student
forced to read nothing but rape literature.

I wrote how he came into college desirous to absorb,
to gain a broad spectrum of literary ideas,
but was forced to bend over instead.
Class after class, only rape. You must read rape.
You must write rape! You must be raped! Or else...
No A.
He cries, "No, I don't want to any more."
And the teacher forces him to.
I write how his literary education gets hijacked,
book by book and essay by essay,
by every woman in creative writing classes
who know that the way to an A is to write about
sex, or assault, or losing virginity to her prom date.
I wrote about the loss of joy in other literature.
Yes, rape is important study in literature,
yet no Frankenstein ethics? No Hemingway icebergs?
No Shakespeare innuendo? Just evil daddies with little girls?
And bad men who take what's most sacred?
And all men are bad! That's why they don't get As,
And I wrote how this college student—class after class
after class after class—
after class—
was tired of all the rape.
And he watched women celebrate it for an A,
even fake it, screaming:
"Yes, Professors! Yes! Make me your valedictorian!"
Yet he grew leery that his education was passing,
that he'd only know that penetrative act that roared:
"You take it! You take it! And you shut up and fake it!
Or you don't get an A."
And I titled the piece: "The Rape."
Turned it in,
and got F-ed again.

Flush

No one cares what you're selling, so long as it looks good. Polish a turd, it's still a turd, but now people want to buy it. Teach it to speak, and now we laugh. Teach it to reason, and we may agree. Teach it to be ambiguous, and we unite as one and all. . . . rolling in it. Then, Teach it to make a joke, and we don't mind. . . Give it a purpose, and we will heartily support it. give it a platform, and it can face off against another great turd. Because some people like turds with a different polish. But then give it some time, and we'll vote for ours, ignoring the stains, the stench, the clogs— the truest vulgarity. Give it voice, and it will play the sweet rose garden, selling greenest meadows and not manure that it really is. Then give it power, and we'll act surprised there's a turd on the throne. Smell the turd stink up the world, and we'll eat what it's serving and then pretend we didn't block the pipes.

Empty Rooms
(a.k.a. Jealous)

A stranger lay in a hospital, alone—
no nurse, no comfort.
And people yelled, "Hooray!"
A doctor fought to save a life—
alone, without extra hands.
And people applauded the death.
A woman needed to walk,
but there was no hand to hold her up.
We laughed when she fell.
A man couldn't hear,
and there was no one to raise the volume.
So, we didn't have to whisper our jokes.
An earthquake hit a building.
It fell, and no one knew why.
And the rubble didn't bother us.
Criminals embezzled from the people.
They got away because no one even knew.
That's just how money works.
Children grew into morons
because there was no one to pass on knowledge.
Which is okay, because teachers are evil.
A mother and child needed protection,
but all the offices were empty.
So, she had to stay married to their bruises.
When I pointed this out,
a friend said, "you're just jealous."
Apparently, he thinks his life will
never have bumps.
I hope he's right.
The rest of us will just have to live
in the real and lonelier world now.
Which I tried to tell him,
but he couldn't understand
because he studied film and marketing
instead of humanity.

World of Dragons

And it came to pass the dragon fought against God.
The dragon was an idiot, so he fought against choice.
He thought he could be God.

He said, "listen to me, and I will act as a savior.
I will cause everyone to make the right decision."
He said, "then you will call me just as God."

Then a lamb raised his voice and asked: "may I go forth?
I will be savior, and give you free will.
And I will give credit to God."

Then the dragon rebelled,
when two-thirds wanted choice.
So, the dragon took his third to hell.

"Yay! We're righteous," cheered the winners.
"We have won to have choice."
Then they came to Earth to eat veal and tell others what to do.

A Story for Children

I don't have a screaming conscience,
but I know what right and wrong. . .

. . . IS.

I've never been good at memorizing scripture, but I recall how Christ...

I don't claim to be a holy person,
but I've never prayed to. . .

So when I watch you cheer at breaking others,
I wonder where you found your...

. . . faith?

For Beatitudes and Spacious Skies.

1. His disciples came.
2. And opened their ears and heard Him say

Blessed are the poor in spirit, for they can't partake in our riches.

Blessed are they that mourn, for they shall be comforted elsewhere.

Blessed are the meek for they shall inherit a return trip home.

Blessed are they which do hunger and thirst, the desert is plentiful.

Blessed are the merciful, for they assign all of the window seats.

Blessed are the pure in heart, for they shall feel righteous for now.

Blessed are the peacemakers, for laws let them shun and neglect.

Blessed are they which are persecuted for righteousness sake, for theirs is the kingdom left by selfish zealots.

Blessed are ye, when men shall revile you, and persecute you, and shall say evil against you falsely.

Blessed are ye, for now you can be sent off to be forgotten and never worry about having to pay your dues.

Blessed are ye, and be exceeding glad: for great is your reward on your side of the border, where God dwells.

Blessed is your side of the border, for God's side of the border is love, and our side's too righteous for God.

Blessed are the salt of the earth: for if the salt have lost his savour, the food will rot. And God throws it out.

Wood Coaster Rhythm

For those of you now boarding,
please check your privilege
until it locks firmly against your being.
If it does not lock firmly against your being,
please raise your hand
and a soulless profiteer will teach you how to bully.

Welcome to life!
Please keep your thoughts and opinions to yourself.
Always conform.
Please get offended.
And have violence!

Here's your syllabus!
Please turn to page one and follow with me.
Okay, NOW:

Don't frown.
Don't joke.
Don't drink.
Don't smoke.
Can't smile.
Can't play.
Can't be white.
Can't be gay.
No blacks.
No browns.
No heres.
No out of towns.
Block voice!
Team up.
Make groups.
Build gangs.
Cliques!

Wait for it. . .

Try.
Fail!
Pass.
Cheat.
Close your mind, know your place.
Memorize. Regurgitate.

We
now
shut
down
people who
disagree with you, and

Grow
old.
Get
mad
that the youth
don't care for you.
Scream
loud.
Last
breath!

Die. . .

Welcome back!
Please remain seated until you can identify
just what you think you accomplished.
Please get out! And thank you for wasting everyone's time.

Prisoner LCCN 31035230

Sing! Oh. Sing, sweet Mnemosyne:
mother of muses,
literature, science and arts.
Reinvigorate the spirit of Appolodorus.
Aid us to dwell in the fatherhood of his prison
and his intentions for who should not escape.
For instance, those Puritans
and their New English Canaan,
of which only 25 souls still breathe.
Pray! Let loose this remaining discord.
And tell us not of that devastating day in 1884,
when 31035230 was born.
Instead, wisk us—oh Mnemosyne—
to a far safer time,
to wiser generations that have forgotten such danger,
to when prisons ignored bigots and moral crusaders.
Take us a hundred years, take us more
to the 1990s when prisons were darker than today's.
And we tried to release
scary stories and Daddy's roommate
from Terabithian bridges and their purple color.
And we tossed straw hats and mice and men and sex and
31035—what the stars and shadows?
Not far enough, Mnemosyne! He's still caged!
Take us ten years more for this criminal's demise.
Surely, sing! Muses, daughters of Mnemosyne!
Your voices silenced by fear and modernity:
help your mother remind us
how her children were misled by
captains of underpants,
and the perks they lost from being wallflowers
when they were off killing mockingbirds!
Why? Because you got goosebumps
when you heard the roll of thunder
and got scorched in heats of 451.

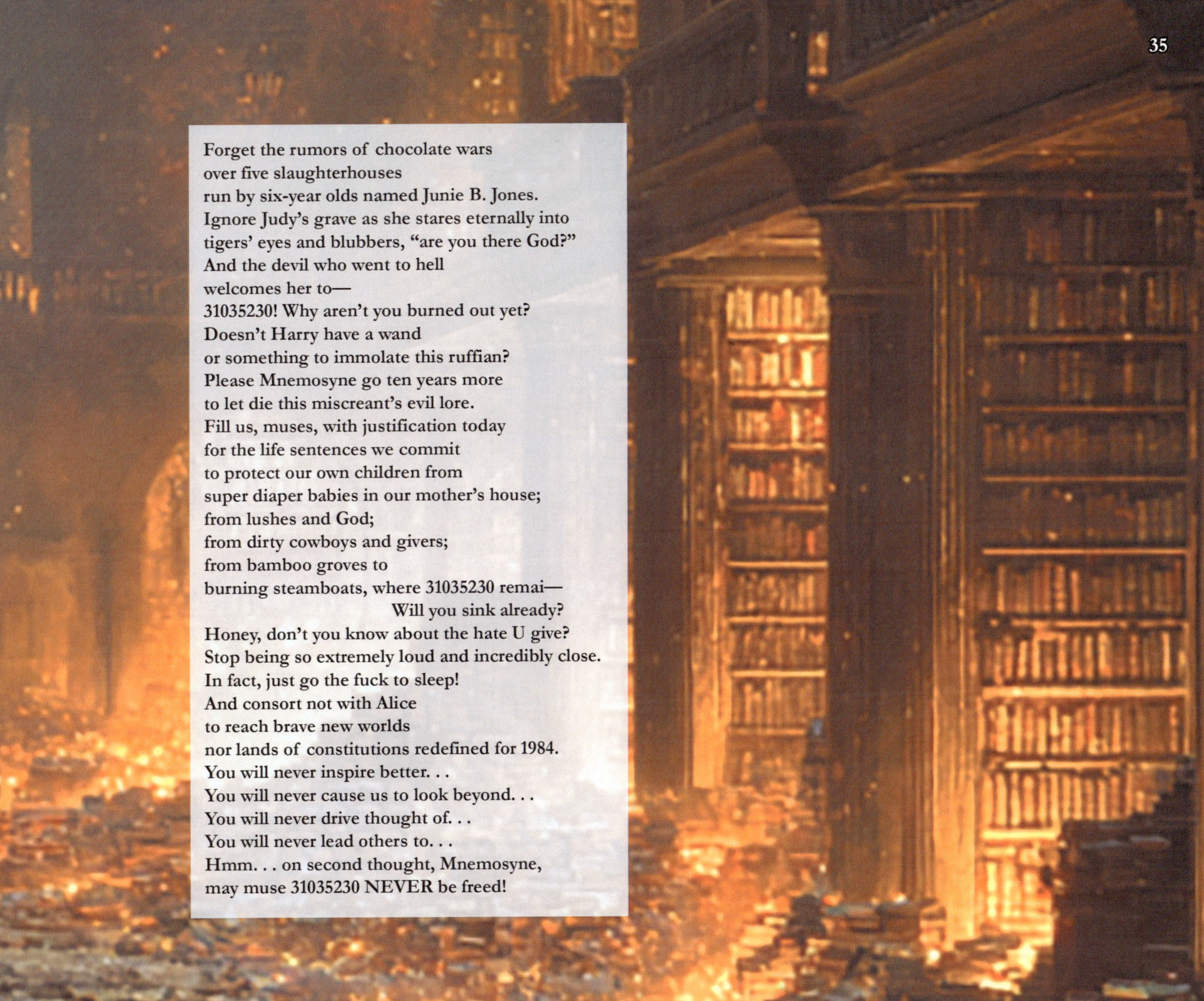

Forget the rumors of chocolate wars
over five slaughterhouses
run by six-year olds named Junie B. Jones.
Ignore Judy's grave as she stares eternally into
tigers' eyes and blubbers, "are you there God?"
And the devil who went to hell
welcomes her to—
31035230! Why aren't you burned out yet?
Doesn't Harry have a wand
or something to immolate this ruffian?
Please Mnemosyne go ten years more
to let die this miscreant's evil lore.
Fill us, muses, with justification today
for the life sentences we commit
to protect our own children from
super diaper babies in our mother's house;
from lushes and God;
from dirty cowboys and givers;
from bamboo groves to
burning steamboats, where 31035230 remai—
              Will you sink already?
Honey, don't you know about the hate U give?
Stop being so extremely loud and incredibly close.
In fact, just go the fuck to sleep!
And consort not with Alice
to reach brave new worlds
nor lands of constitutions redefined for 1984.
You will never inspire better...
You will never cause us to look beyond...
You will never drive thought of...
You will never lead others to...
Hmm... on second thought, Mnemosyne,
may muse 31035230 NEVER be freed!

Why the People?

Is this not what we wanted?

Lots of images of anger and hate?
And I have to wonder why people are so surprised.

When all we exercise are "Terms of Use" policies,
and neglect practicing the freedoms of the Constitution.
And then people do wrong?
I wonder why we are surprised.

When we confuse "Terms of Use" with the concept of freedom,
stifle our own maintenance of humane progression;
and encourage a society that oppresses ourselves
so it can lock away others,
I wonder why we are surprised.

"Terms of Use" sustains profits,
not people, not freedom.

Observe the foundation of life, liberty and happiness:
right to protest, assemble, the freedom to speak.
Guarantee of just trial. Free to walk your own street!
Free from tyranny in law and those who enforce.

While "Terms of Use" ensure power through followers
. . . or tyrants.
It depends on your needs.
Court of public opinion?
Silence a protest?
Pretend people can speak,
but don't let them upset?
We practice these in social media,
but it's only ugly on streets?
And I wonder why we are surprised.

The horse at the cart has been laughing at how little we see.
As tourism has become influencers screaming, "look at me!"
And moderators get more respect than police,
because they're drowning in ice.

When we become comfortable
With irresponsibility and neglect,
how can we be surprised at the behaviors we see,
If we do not stop them through the practice of Constitutional decree?
People say, "we are a nation of laws,"
as an excuse to hate, to oppress, to exclude,
and then are surprised when those targets react.

A "nation of law" means involvement of voice,
not just at the ballot, but when we know laws neglect.
Laws do neglect.
Hence, the purpose for voice:
in letters to leaders;
to government makers;
to public-official, watchdog groups
that are less likely to profit from "Terms of Use."
Why can we rally voices in personal outcry,
but we can't take them to offices of lawmakers?

Why?

Is it because we *must* have a villain?
Someone or something to be angry at?
And we must see that place where false fault falls?
That is how "Terms of Use" thrives.
Someone must be the cause.
If we are shocked at what we see,
while we neglect freedoms and civic duty;
interact with "Terms of Use,"
rather than exercise the Constitution,
we forget!
We badly behave.
We contribute to others who badly behave.
And that is what villains do,
is it not?
And when we do as villains do,
and see people behave in the streets,
as we behave with "Terms of Use,"
I have no choice but wonder, is this not what we wanted?

Nation Of Laws

We are a nation of laws founded in the dowery of compassion,
grounded in the mercies of "all men are created equal."
It was branded in the voices of leaders who saw their fellow man struggling
and said, "we must make our laws see her."
We are a nation of laws founded in the savageness of war.
In bloodshed did we trust to ensure the nobility of man without oppression.
And the motto of "give me your tired, your poor, your huddled masses"
was 'cuz we needed help to kick everyone's asses, so we could stay.
And the mother of exile is a prisoner, forgotten in name, imagined in wonder,
frozen in shock that her Lazarus may rise to cry,
"we are a nation of laws, baptized in the waters of diversity,
and confirmed in the spirit that Ben Franklin called a bully."
It's one that douses the torch,
one that corrupts the land beneath the podium.
We stole it from others, with deadly talons,
just like the bald eagle that relishes in garbage and steals others' food.
We robbed noblemen by pretending them unholy.
It was law, and voices ensured their extinction—
because we are a nation of laws, of awe, of what our forefathers saw,
which was the preservation of love that men of power are created better.

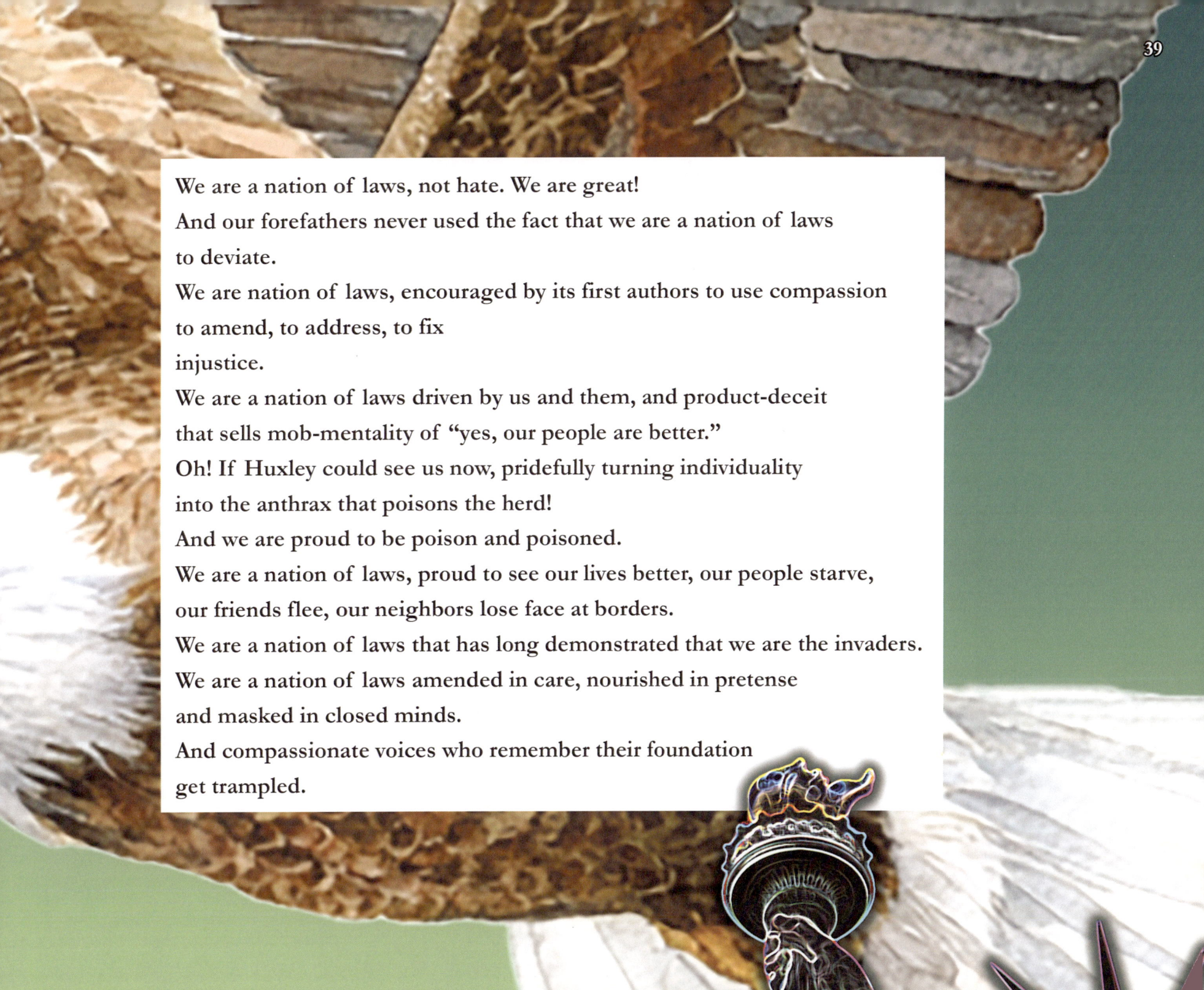

We are a nation of laws, not hate. We are great!
And our forefathers never used the fact that we are a nation of laws
to deviate.
We are nation of laws, encouraged by its first authors to use compassion
to amend, to address, to fix
injustice.
We are a nation of laws driven by us and them, and product-deceit
that sells mob-mentality of "yes, our people are better."
Oh! If Huxley could see us now, pridefully turning individuality
into the anthrax that poisons the herd!
And we are proud to be poison and poisoned.
We are a nation of laws, proud to see our lives better, our people starve,
our friends flee, our neighbors lose face at borders.
We are a nation of laws that has long demonstrated that we are the invaders.
We are a nation of laws amended in care, nourished in pretense
and masked in closed minds.
And compassionate voices who remember their foundation
get trampled.

Life Logic

How can one argue, "my body my choice,"
at the cost of another's body and their choice?

Why not just say you don't want it?
At least that's a founded argument?

How can one say, "you're a murderer,"
when rape's already stolen a life?

Why can't nunyas admit that, in extremes,
one's business dies while one gets to live?

Seems more gets to live between extremes.

How can one use science to delay when life starts,
when science defines life as "it's not dead?"
Is that a zombie growing large in the womb?

Yet, how can one say there's no excuse and no mercy
in the name of He who says that there is?
Why do Christians always remember fire and brimstone,
but drop requirements to judge not, and forgive?

Why must we stand here, or must we stand there,
when there are many flagstones in between?

How can we keep standing, when our logic keeps falling?
Is it that hard to live your own life?
To worry about your own sins?

Seems I already have one God looking out for mine,
and I don't remember you being Him.

Sticks and Stones

What ever happened to the concept of thought?
Individuality thinking?
People with brains—
now, rocks.
Sticks and stones break amendments.
Crash!
Republican't. Demoncrat.
Uneducated with baseball bats!
Loud mouths who carry straw.
Suppression of choice.
Violation of voice.
Help!
Rape!
I'm offended.
Facts now ever harm me.

Heroes

Where have all the heroes gone?
The leader who was a soldier?
The diplomat who persuaded a king?
The author who died near his frenemy?
The little man who helped father Constitution?
The engineer of borders and states?
The "Old Man Eloquent" and the "atrocious saint?"
The natural born who stopped growth of slavery?
The short-lived champion of the Northwest?
The one who defined rules for the runner up?
The master communicator?
The one who was above politics?
The bandage that held a broken union at borders?
The wimp who still tried?
The hunter and liberator of slave ships?
The theater enthusiast who preserved us, but not himself?
The rabid, mouse-sized mind who befriended China?
The African-American ally-general who stomped that rodent?
The one who fought exclusion?
The martyr who might have continued that fight?

The reunifier?
The one who courted and won Lady Liberty?
The silver Midas?
The Lady's favorite returned?
The one killed for modernizing and growth?
The one with a big stick?
The pitcher?
The father of mother's day?
The one who funded maternal and child care?
The bridge between notarieties?
The volunteer?
The new dealer?
The desegregationist?
The one who painted a target on the moon?
The one who kept safety and war?
The one who brought the boys home?
The national champion and MVP?
The peace broker?
The actor and rebuilder of homes and dreams?
The Texas Senior?
The trader?
The Texas warrior?
The Grammy and Nobel winner?
The one who kicked the gameboard when he lost!
The old winner who just couldn't win?
The one who [CENSORED]

INFLUENCER

It's not all about you, you whiney, little snit.
Slaves sell sex, and you peddle their lipstick.
You don't get cheese, so you stream Karen.
The truth is, before your first like,
someone should have posted
that the fry cook's more needed than you.

Beware, All Ye Who Enter

Off the top of my head,
I can't imagine why I would let anyone
in, nor why others try to let others into theirs.
I don't know why anyone would want to get inside
my head and read or decode any of that useless writing.
On these Here is chaos. In this Here is loss. Within my
walls, Within my dark, skull, gory albatross! idle brain,
there is Feel my logic there break its seams. there's a
nothing. Hear my icy are scars. screams! darkness.
And they all play a W trick H on all ye who near.
to break promise h of a o   road that never
ends, that never y had an w exit or escape.
Wo unto them who strive to know! Are
you sure you want to? Because I live
here, and   I cannot   get out!
I cannot   find the   door.
I did   warn   you.

Colors of Hell

Today, everyone thinks they're abused.
An unkind word lingers.
It fingers.
It pokes at ego,
molding as clay.
So, it stays
in your mind that its bad;
that you had a sad life,
full of strife.
Yet you don't know spit!
So, you play,
in your way,
that you have a clue.
You stand high
as you try
to ride the coattails
of those who've been hit;
who've been bit;
who've been struck
with belts,
leaving welts,
or with boards
that smash
and bash. . . your ass.
You pretend to be sick.
And you lie,
while others die.
You know the words that hurt,
but not the tones
that break bones.

You raise your glass to say,
"Look at me
and see
I'm popular hashtag too!"
And it's a game
to your name
to gaslight your followers and friends.
You pretend to be bent
on the car with that dent
when you weren't, but it feels good
with that mic
and the likes
that bring in the dough.
But reality dies
in your bed of lies.
And you deserve your own hell.

The Bell

In all history
and all war,
the bell started each round.

It predicated all
slavery, genocide, oppression—
gave permission to bully and lessen.

It is the easiest knee-jerk reaction to have.
It's one that we choose,
one we give power.

It's not in the Constitution,
nor its amendments,
nor bills.

It's not a right,
nor a code.
It's the coward's shelter from forgiving.

The fathers of our founding fathers fought against it!
They were targets.
That's why they left to become refugees.

It is a means to puff up;
an excuse to blame;
an entitled blade in the back of society.

We fear it!
It invites silence.
It is the enemy to the evolution of thought.

Hallelujah!

We embrace it.
We sustain it,
though it fights against the betterment of community.

It burns families,
and countries.
Its ash rolls as undying lava across dead seas.

Who cares who cures cancer?
Or promotes world peace?
We'd rather remain viral.

It is easy.
It is poison.
It is fame.

I could tell you what it is.
I would fall on deaf ears.
It rings loudly already, which is what we want to hear.

Spectacles

A precipice for children—
not most, just those—
who subscribe to daddy's call.

A place for they who falter
who cry, who sob,
who fail when mommy's wrong.

A history full of poetry:
not great, not clean,
but on the refrigerator door.

A substitute for trophies!
"You are perfect.
Let none cancel your show."

"We know your thoughts are righteous,
for they are ours.
So reject revisions otherwise, my child, my light."

And the old man sits at the front of the class—
his spectacles in his hand,
for what he's seen, and what he's done,
and his perspectives from the past.

And the old man says, "here, try these on."
And the child says, "go to hell!
Just give my A and Play-doh on a tray.
And that paper that says I am done."

The old man goes home, and dies a little that night
to youth's treason. And his season has passed.
His glasses are lost.

And the child, all knowing,
thanks mom and dad.

Human Shield

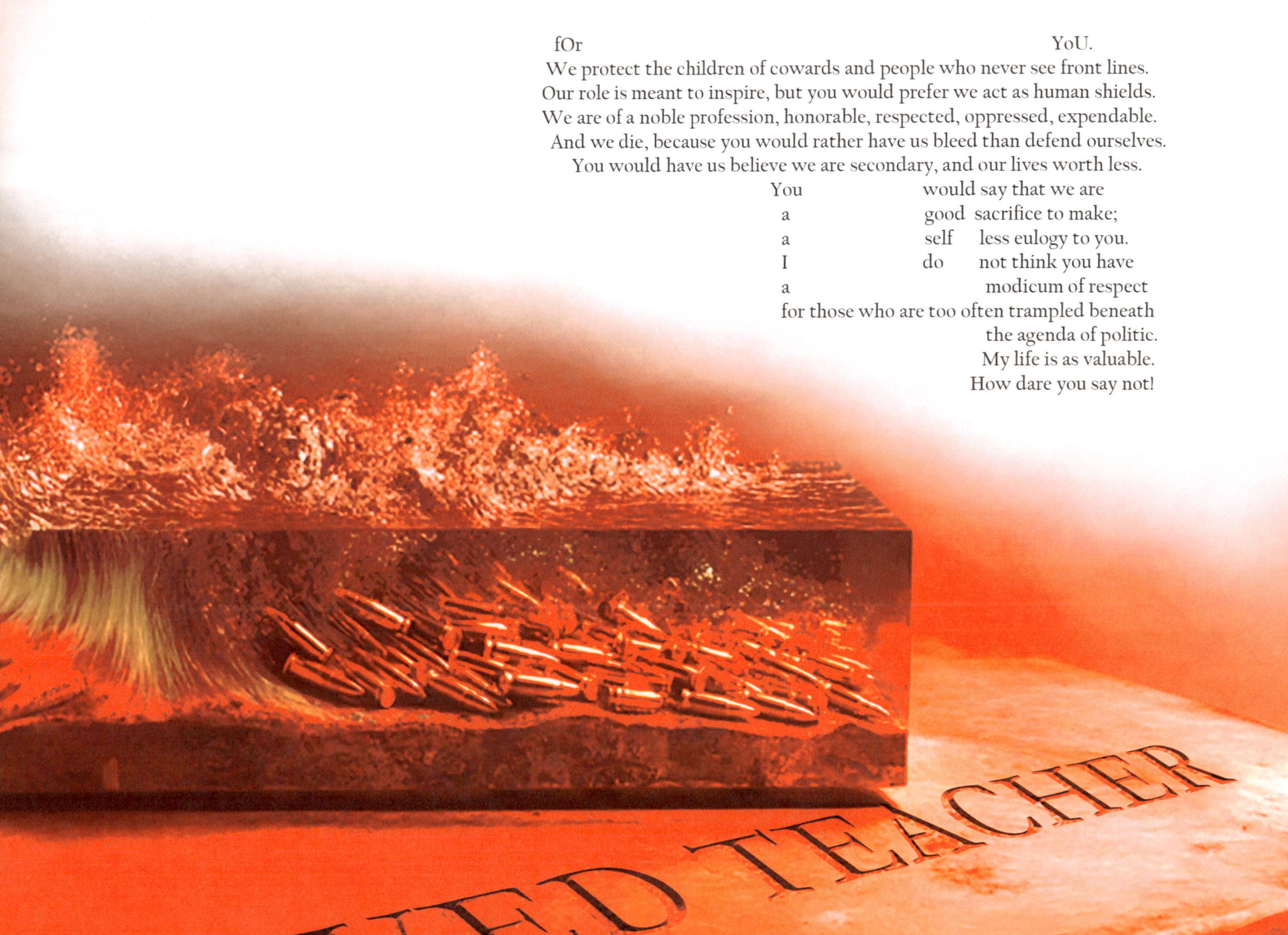

fOr YoU.
We protect the children of cowards and people who never see front lines.
Our role is meant to inspire, but you would prefer we act as human shields.
We are of a noble profession, honorable, respected, oppressed, expendable.
And we die, because you would rather have us bleed than defend ourselves.
You would have us believe we are secondary, and our lives worth less.

    You   would say that we are
    a   good sacrifice to make;
    a   self   less eulogy to you.
    I   do   not think you have
    a   modicum of respect

for those who are too often trampled beneath
the agenda of politic.
My life is as valuable.
How dare you say not!

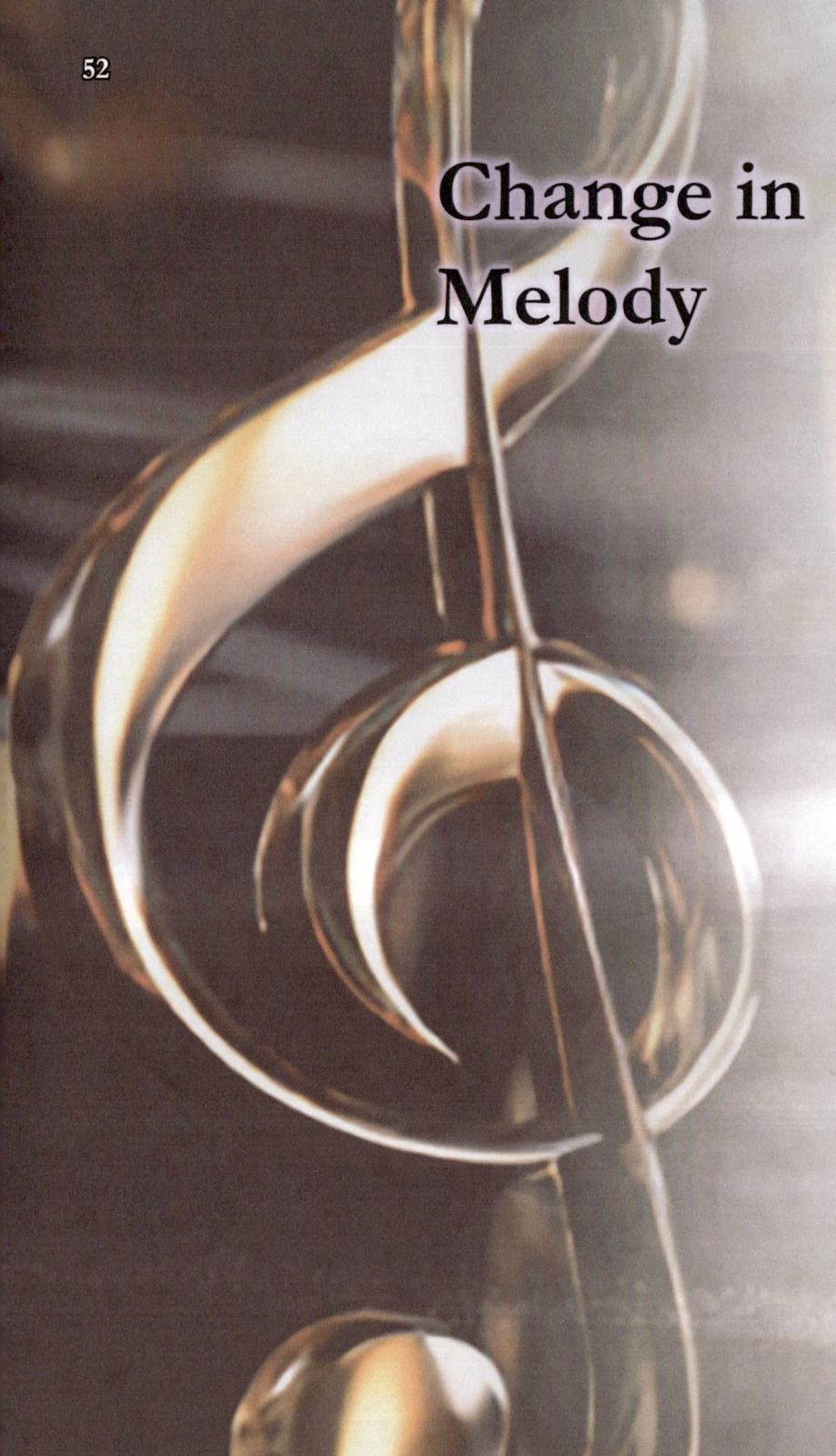

Change in Melody

Music wafting in the morning:
ivory keys and student's hands.
Mother counting down the hallway,
"One and two and three and four and."
Back to the start to play anew,
fingers stroke the musical glands
through the measure. Oops! A mistake!
"One and two and three and four and."
 Legato then into ritard;
"One and two and three and four and!"
Staccato then tremolo.
"One and two and three and four and."
"One and two and three and four and."
"One and two and three and four and!"
Accelerando. Con Brio!
One and two and three and four and—

Chord!

Because the chord is life:
with harmony, to melody
and all around;
To that one note that rhymes with three
simple strings that all have their own chime.

One. . .
and two. . .
and three. . .
and four. . .

and rest, because your fingers are in pain.
Crack your knuckles.
Change the sheet.
Try something by John Barry.

But your fingers ache,
And your rhythm cries,
And your brain screams,
And your heart? Well, it dies.

And the piano falls silent in the morning.
No more Star Wars.
No more Born Free.
Ice Castles melt,
And Brian stops singing.

The American Hero can't fly.

But his fingers still play
Somewhere in Time,
because that's where it's etched into your being.

Every morning,
Somewhere in Time:
the memory lingers, that melody, that composition
of the pupil's chord that touches hearts;
that gives life;
that teaches the lame to walk;
that overcomes rage;
that learns to write symphonies in the key of love;
all because he learned how to make a hammer kiss a string. . .
and make a note.

And the note lingers
even after it diminishes.

And the master, who has heard every hymn,
heals the student's fingers and says,
"One and two and three and four and. . .

Heavenly Pickets

I once asked a man if he could ask God
anything he wanted, what would it be.
At once, his head twisted in contempt,
and he said:
"I would ask God why people have to suffer!
I would ask what kind of a God allows a child to die.
I would ask God where he gets off letting
criminals find success while the innocent pay.
I would look God square in his face and say,
'how dare he!'
I would ask god why there's plague, famine and pain.
I would ask god what he's ever done to stop it."
Then he asked if I had any more stupid questions.
And I said, "just one.
What have you ever done to stop it?"

A man once complained about how
we don't do more for the poor.
He railed on taxes he thought
more people should pay:
"I'd gladly pay more if it meant
taking care of those in need," he claimed.
And I asked, "so, what's stopping you?"

A woman once sat on a street and shouted,
"God's unfair! God's unfair! Who is he to judge me?"
Then a car struck her,
and I wonder if she ever got her answer.

A man once complained that a church had money.
I said, "maybe they're saving it for a party."

A friend once asked, "do you know why
I don't like your faith?"
And I answered, "well, what you believe is
really none of my business, now is it?"

A student once asked what I thought
was the biggest difference between
her generation and mine
And I said, "you mean besides the diapers?"

After a difficult day, a peer asked
what I thought the definition of
sanity was, and I said,
"accepting that you can't make everyone happy."

A teenager asked what
entitlement was,
and I said, "pretending God's just your sugar daddy."

I once had an undergraduate class ask how I could be proud
of the world I was leaving them.
And I said, "well, I'd feel a lot better about it if you'd stop
wasting it on junk that breaks every month."

I once asked my next-door neighbor:
"how do you deal with all the
self-righteous and dumb people in the world?"
And he said, "well, fences help."

Pop Quiz

I said:
Love thy enemy.
Love thy neighbor.
Forgive until 7 times 70.
Of you it is required to forgive everyone.
And I will forgive whom I will.
Judge not. I will judge.
Give him your coat.
Suffer the children.
Whoever is least is greatest.
The greatest among you is like the ruler who serves.
Doing unto the least is doing unto me.
And while I'm at it,
I will heal your ear.
I will heal the sinners,
and lower class,
refugees,
the faithless,
ungrateful,
and dead.
I will break bands of death to complete you.
My mission is to save lives, not destroy them.

Question :

In a world where you knew my teachings;
In a world where you were well-versed;
In a world where you claimed to know me;
But my lessons, instead, you perversed;
When I have to come back to correct things;
Who do you think I'm gonna slap to fix first?

Light at the End of the Tunnel

What if I'm wrong?
What if my new supervisor was right that day
when he walked in, tore down the poster of policies
and said, "we're not doing this any more!"
What if all that heartache his predecessor caused
to build her ego, to sustain her power,
was only temporary?
What if all that crying and doomsday-thought
that said our workplace would never be the same
could have been avoided if we'd have just remembered:
in with the new and out with the old?
Why are we so eager to be walked all over?
And forget that someone else will come along
to lift us back up?
Why are we so short-sighted to see a championship trophy
and think it will be the last one someone will ever win?
Four becomes three.
Three becomes two.
Two becomes one.
And one becomes someone else
who walks in and says,
"Yeah. . . we're not doing this anymore!"

Try

Who cares about roses?
They're easy.
They never die.
They NEVER leave!
Smell the poppies—subtle.
Blink, and they're gone.
Try skipping.
Watch a cloud, or two,
or spend an hour's worth
listening to a creek giggle.
Find the bird that's hunting.
Fall asleep to leaves playing
or the wind-puppy that licks your face.
Whistling! Start whistling
while mowing the lawn.
And who cares what others say?
It's not their lawn.
Pay compliment in an elevator,
Sing in a store.
Dance to the escalator,
or right where you are.
Walk, just walk.
Or run.
Or bike.

Drive. Take the dog.
Take a lunch.
Turn right instead of left.
See where you find yourself.
Leave the phone behind.
Breathe. . .
Breathe. . .
The world's not ending.
Don't miss it living
while focusing on how it's dying.
Plant a tree.
Tell a joke.
Listen to children play.
But stay out of their playground.
No one built it for you to ruin.
For no reason,
take a train.
ride a bus.
Soar!
Say hi to the person next to you,
and ask if they've seen a more beautiful day.
Or you can keep finding fault
and blaming your neighbors,
but who ever smiles that way?

Benediction

Now, I lay me down to sleep,
a "child of God" watches my feet.
If I should go before I wake,
you'll know that bastard took me away.

Fairchild teaches university composition. He remains a lifelong-learner and Christian (for those who draw the wrong assumption). He is a strong supporter of the Constitution and opposes any behavior that robs another person of choice, of voice, or uses hate to impose actions upon others. He has worked extensively in amusement and entertainment and is the author of the award winning books *Boom*, *The Exodus*, and *Steering Classes off Cliffs: 10 Ways Professors Sabotage Students to Crash and Burn* (which he co-wrote with author and former student Elyse Kunzler).

Other books By David Fairchild

The Exodus

Boom

Jello Freeways: 10 Ways Students Sabotage Their Efforts (Campus Nightmares Vol. 1)

Steering Classes off Cliffs: 10 Ways Professors Sabotage Students to Crash and Burn (Campus Nightmares Vol. 2)

Where's the Blood

Circle of Dogs: The New Paladin

Circle of Dogs: Wolf

Circle of Dogs: Eulogies

www.ingramcontent.com/pod-product-compliance
Lightning Source LLC
Chambersburg PA
CBRC102029050526
44107CB00112B/1277